CURTIN CALL

CURTIN CALL

A Photographer's Candid View of 25 Years of Music in Canada

WALTER CURTIN

*Jon Vickers in his
dressing room at the
Bavarian State Opera
in Munich, 28
September 1975.*

*(Opposite) Lilian
Sukis in Verdi's* Luisa
Miller *at the Vienna
State Opera,
2 October 1975.*

Exile Editions

This edition is published by
Exile Editions Limited,
20 Dale Avenue Toronto,
Ontario, Canada M4W 1K4

SALES DISTRIBUTION
General Publishing Co. Ltd.,
30 LesMill Road, Don Mills,
Ontario M3B 2T6

*T*his book is dedicated to my wife,
the painter, Isabel Kann, and our
extensions in time, Katie, Joseph,
John, Mary, Caroline, and Philippa

ACKNOWLEDGMENTS
This publication was supported by
The Socan Foundation

The Samuel and Saidye Bronfman
Family Foundation

Photos from the Walter Curtin Collection at
the National Archives of Canada, Ottawa

John Curtin

Design by Ken Rodmell

Printed by Best Book Manufacturers Inc.

(Endpapers)
'The Dream Concert of the
Decade' at Toronto's Massey
Hall, 17 November 1974,
with tenor Jon Vickers,
soprano Birgit Nilsson,
bass William Wilderman,
and conductor Zubin Mehta
with The Toronto Symphony.

Contents

Foreword

John Reeves

WALTER CURTIN IS A VIENNESE in the way Charles Boyer was a Parisian. Born in August, 1911, in Vienna, Walter is a phenomenally charming, very sociable man. His finest photographs are of people, perhaps because his social skills are among his keenest photographic tools. In fact, Walter's whole life could be viewed as one long considerate gesture to which his accumulated works stand as a monument. Essentially, there are two kinds of photographers: those who seem to "make" photographs by manipulating people and objects in front of the camera, and those who more or less "find" photographs by manipulating themselves and their cameras in front of people and objects. "I search for my pictures," explains Walter. "I believe that I'm the one who should be moving around, not my subjects." He sees photography as an information gathering and transmitting tool and has little patience with "arty"photographs that seem to be about nothing but photography itself: form without content. Introduce yourself as a "photo artist" and start talking about your "images" and the impeccably courteous Curtin will capitulate to a compelling urge to take his dog for a walk.

It took some time for photography to become the centre of Walter's life. As Walter Spiegel, his early career focussed on business interests in Vienna. Walter's family was Jewish and owned a substantial food wholaling company which he managed from his father's death in 1933 until 1938 when, with the growth of Nazi anti-semitism, he and his brother decided to leave Austria. During

Walter and Arthur Davidson, conductor. London, October 28, 1975

7

his last months in Vienna he studied photoengraving and worked for a Viennese portrait photographer with the thought that he should acquire a practical skill to make him readily employable in a new country.

In March 1939, the Spiegel brothers were allowed to go to England to await permission to emigrate to the United States. The next few years of Walter's life were very much determined by the onset of the Second World War. In England, he worked at whatever he could find—first as a tea boy in a factory and then as an oil-burner service apprentice. On the day war was declared, both he and his brother volunteered for service in the British Army. They were rejected as "Aliens". Now out of work, Walter drew unemployment benefits while attending trade school in London to study color printing. When France fell in 1940, he and his brother found themselved interned in a camp for Aliens and then shipped to Australia.

In the middle of their 56-day voyage, Winston Churchill announced that it was now acceptable for "friendly aliens" to join the British Army. But at this point, there was no choice but to sail on to Australia. To help pass the time there, Walter and his fellow aliens formed a very undersupplied but very enthusiastic photographic club.

1941 found the brothers back in England and in the army at last. Walter was advised that Curtin was a better name than Spiegel in the event of his possible capture. The capture-proof Curtin's photographic inclinations had to remain dormant until his discharge in 1946 when he was able to persuade the Studio Sun in London to accept him as an apprentice. The studio was an exciting place to be. Walter found himself surrounded by other highly-motivated veterans, all eager to make up for the war's intrusion into their lives.

He worked at developing color films, mixing the chemicals to process them himself. The Studio Sun did a lot of business photographing works of art for books, and Curtin soon found himself behind a camera copying paintings. In1948, he left the Studio, borrowed money from some friends and set up his own shop in an unused scullery in Kensington. He became renowned for the technical quality of his work and soon attracted TIME and TIME LIFE BOOKS as clients for his impeccably executed photographs of paintings and objects d'art. Travelling extensively in both England and Europe, he began to meet other photographers, among them Henri Cartier-Bresson, Dimitri Kessel, Kryn Taconis, and the Cappa Brothers (Robert and Cornell). Walter, the Viennese food broker, found himself immersed in the world of art and photography.

His career in London continued until 1952 when an economic recession in Britain prompted a move to Canada (which seemed a lot more inviting than the United States, where McCarthyism was in full swing). At this time, Walter wanted to change more than his address; the photographers who were his friends and whose work he had come to admire most—men like Kessel and Taconis—were photojournalists who had grown up under the influence of the "tween" the Great Wars founders of modern "candid" photojournalism—photographers such as Eric Salomon and André Kertesz. Kessel and Taconis took pictures full of people and events that were imbued with (to misquote Cartier-Bresson slightly) "that precise organization of forms which gives those events their proper expressions." Six years of photographing paintings had taught Walter to love art but not necesssarily the process of reproducing it. He had also learned to love an artist, Isabel Kann, whom he married in November, 1949. Now, when his visual sensibilities needed stroking, he could talk to his wife. He still does.

When he started looking for work in Toronto, Walter represented himself not as Curtin the color craftsman but as Curtin the photojournalist. His first Canadian magazine assignment addressed to this new, creative, persona was a portrait in 1953 of the hockey legend, King Clancy, for the cover of *Liberty* magazine. In the same year, the National Film Board hired Walter as a still photographer for a film called *The Stratford Adventure*. He managed to take some memorable pictures of the Stratford Festival's founding director, Tyrone Guthrie, while perfecting his skills with small cameras and fast black and white film. Curtin's photo essays became very visible in major Canadian magazines, including *Maclean's*, *Weekend* and *Chatelaine*.

Gradually, Walter had evolved from a large-camera craftsman to a small-camera virtuoso. Disliking the use of flash, he equipped himself with Nikon SP rangefinder cameras and became very much an available light photographer. He was quick to start using "hot" film developers like Acufine and then the new Diafine to boost the speed of his basic film material, Tri-X, from 400 to 800 ASA.

By the late 1950s, Curtin's Viennese sociability and his knack for photographing "real" people, started to attract advertising clients. When he returned to England for a few years in 1963, he produced, among other things, a remarkable advertising campaign for Wills cigars. Divorced from the client's message, the photographs for Wills stand up beautifully as a collection of genre portraits: the people in these pictures are real (Curtin does not like to use professional models), but if you look twice, all are smoking a cigar.

Another British economic recession prompted Curtin's return to Toronto in 1968, and he continued to freelance here. As an admirer of *A Private View*, Lord Snowdon's photographic record of contemporary British visual artists and their milieu, published in 1965, he decided to start documenting Canadian musicians. Three of his six children studied music, and their enthusiasm led to the recognition of a need for a book that would project the richness of the Canadian classical and serious contemporary music scene.

Walter embarked on his musical project in 1972 and the work soon became something of an obsession. He haunted music schools, rehearsal halls, concert venues and artists' homes. His collection of portraits grew and by 1982 there was more than enough material for a substantial book but the book just didn't quite happen. God knows the project was perceived as important and it attracted important supporters. The emminent composer and scholar, Louis Applebaum, loved what Walter was doing, and so did the outstanding graphic designer, sometime blues singer, jazz trombonist and all-round music lover, Ken Rodmell. The country's most incisive music critic, Kenneth Winters, expressed an enthusiastic interest in producing a text for a portrait collection. But publishers couldn't see a safe way to produce Walter's book. Eleven years went by. An introduction in early 1994 to Walter and his urbane photos enchanted publisher/editor Barry Callaghan. And so, Applebaum, Rodmell, Winters and the enchantable publisher Callaghan found a way to move forward, bringing Curtin's magnificent twenty-two year obsession to splendid fruition. Callaghan is responsible for the book's title *Curtin Call.*

Not every eighty-three year old photographer gets to deliver a magnum opus, replete with fresh new images generated right up until press time. But this book is as it should be. Walter Curtin is one of the greatest exponents of the found (candid) photo portrait. He is a true descendant of Eric Salomon, André Kertesz and Henri Cartier-Bresson. As the book's designer, Rodmell says, "A lot of people will be surprised by these pictures because they're going to see how good this guy really is." Damn right.

MusicVisible

Ken Winters

WALTER CURTIN'S PHOTOGRAPHS of musicians engaged in their lives—that is to say, in their music—are for me like that fateful mouthful of tea and cake ("petite madeleine") in Proust's *A la recherche du temps perdu*. They recapture a rich succession of musical experiences filed away somewhere in myself yet now, prompted by these pictures, so sprung again to life that I can hear them.

The 1960s, '70s, '80s were years of an unprecedented step forward in music in Canada. They gave us our first own parade of stars; our first own generation of composers; our first own substructure of musical livelihoods, which made the rest possible. These years brought the first flourish of a collective identity we may call *not* nationalism (grisly term of bullying exclusions, pompous assumptions of superiority, beastly descents into racial cleansing) but its benign sibling, nationality; an identity with a larger entity than the id. Nationality here bespeaks, perhaps, certain various flavors of taste, certain ways of speaking and acting that grow, in Canada, out of the many encompassed nationalities, (for example, two of our most distinguished pianists, Anton Kuerti, born in Austria, and Antonín Kubálek, born in Czechoslovakia; and two of our best composers, Michael Colgrass, born in the USA, and Harry Freedman, born in Poland). Canadian musicians in the 1960s, '70s and '80s, independent of those unattractive nationalisms that strove to cramp and limit and divide them, did seem to articulate their

Nadia Boulanger at her home and teaching studio in Paris, 16 October 1975.

nationality, in which the ancestral variousness was only a strength. This nationality had nothing snooty or vainglorious about it. It was just there. It reminded me of a remark by the great French music teacher Nadia Boulanger who taught so many Canadians—István Anhalt, John Beckwith, Walter Buczynski, Gabriel Charpentier, Jean Papineau-Couture and dozens of others, including me. One day during a lesson, in the course of a discussion about self-knowledge, Mlle Boulanger said matter-of-factly "I'm a Frenchwoman, so in any country I know where I am. I'm a Catholic, so in any church I know what I believe. I'm a musician, so in any company I have my identity." It was that kind of articulate awareness of the self in a context that was dawning on Canadians. To put it rather simply, in a single instance: the pianist Glenn Gould was never a nationalist—the idea would have appalled him—yet he was in the vanguard of this emerging Canadian musical nationality. Gould was a player utterly unlike any European or US-American of his generation. His nearest rivals among his contemporaries were European: Alfred Brendel and the younger Maurizio Pollini. Both Brendel and Pollini continue today to motor along imposingly in the middle lane, while Gould burned himself out in the stratosphere at fifty. But of the three—the iconoclastic Gould, the Biedermeier Brendel, and (in the apt words of pianist William Aide) "that impassive skyscraper of a pianist" Pollini—it was the quintessentially Canadian Gould who was—and still is, through his recordings—the provocateur, the genius, the spellbinder. In other senses, similar and Canadian differences could be claimed for Gould's compatriots in other musical disciplines in those years—composers Harry Somers and Murray Schafer, soprano Lois Marshall, contralto Maureen Forrester, tenor Jon Vickers, conductor Mario Bernardi. Each of these phenomenal Canadian artists moved unassumingly and easily, at home and abroad. Each was graceful and compelling in his or her distinction.

This kind of assured but unaggressive, un-nationalistic nationality grew in Canadian music, musicians and music-making in the 1960s, '70s and '80s, won or earned for the country by the musicians themselves. Paradoxically, as regards the musicians, it wasn't so much a case of Canada producing them as of them producing Canada. The country began to shine musically in their reflected glory. It was not Canada that took Somers and Schafer, Gould and Bernardi, Vickers and Marshall and Forrester into the larger musical world; it was they who took Canada there. During those same years, though, thanks to the efforts of catalystic and practical souls of music like Louis Applebaum, the possibility of livelihoods was growing in Canada. Till then, the growth had been slow.

When the young Canadian Ernest MacMillan agreed to conduct the Toronto Symphony Orchestra in 1931, he took on the responsibility because he wanted it. But the job did not give him a livelihood then and it never did in the twenty-five years he held it. The first livelihood went to his successor, the European conductor Walter Susskind. The players in English-Canada's foremost orchestra were even slower to gain livelihoods. In 1956 they were still in work only half the year, and for pittance. In 1965, after a long struggle, their season ballooned from 26 weeks to 30, and livelihoods for orchestras began to materialize.

When Victor Feldbrill won the Winnipeg Symphony Orchestra in 1958 he was, I suspect, the first Canadian-born conductor to obtain a livelihood with a Canadian symphony orchestra outside the CBC. Even when the Canadian-born Mario Bernardi came home from London ten years later to form the National Arts Centre Orchestra, the notion of entrusting the leadership of a major orchestra to a born Canadian was a novelty.

The 1960s were thus the virtual beginning of the time when a Canadian-born conductor or instrument-player or singer of superior gifts and training could earn a living in Canada performing. Composers will tell you they had to subsidize their work by other means (and they are right: most of them still do have to). But that has always been so in that highest and most headstrong musical art.

Walter Curtin spotted this confident new swirl of Canadian musical life in the late 1960s and resonated to it. To him, to his merry and thoughtful and questing eyes, the country seemed agog and a-jig over music. Three of his own children were up over their ears in it. The Viennese in Walter himself was soon waltzing to it. In the early 1970s the photographer in him succumbed to the desire to seize the look of it. He found he wanted to catch music in the act, music being made. From then till now, this has been his obsession. The pictures in this book are the merest tip of the iceberg; Curtin has taken thousands. How he and his editorial associates restricted themselves to these few, I can't imagine.

In by far the most of Walter Curtin's photographs—and strikingly in these—we see people not "having their pictures taken." All are deeply preoccupied with something more than themselves or than us. All of them, in these glimpses of their preoccupation, fill my ears and my mind with music.

Nadia Boulanger, that honorary Canadian through her countless pupils, is older here than in my precious year with her, but sitting exactly as she did then for ten hours a day in her studio at 36 rue Ballu, intent on the twelve notes of Western music's chromatic scale that grouped and regrouped themselves in the living, unbounded language that for her transcended all others. The groupings were wondrous, for me, that year, but I remember particularly the day we spent on Haydn's *E minor Sonata*, the notes brimming in her complete attention. The photograph here, of which I have a signed copy as a gift from its maker, is one of my prized possessions.

The Gould photographs are by now icons in the mythology of the century's most provocative pianist. I'm proud also to own a Curtin signed print (dated 1961) of a different still from the St. Clair Avenue series here dated 1963. Every time I go past it I feel I'm in a magnetic field of Bachian polyphony. Gould, more than any human conduit, was our epiphany of Bach.

The marvellous photo of Lois Marshall in full cry summons an unsurpassed feast of song over many years, but especially her Schubert cycles (*Die schöne Müllerin* with Greta Kraus; *Winterreise* with pianist Anton Kuerti) and her devastating performance with Kuerti of Brahms' *Four Serious Songs*, all in the mid-1970s, when her voice had darkened. Never in my experience had there been such singing—except perhaps at a Toronto Symphony Student Concert one afternoon, when Ms Marshall shook us with arias of Verdi and Puccini, or, some years later, when she tossed off Purcell's "Hark the echoing air" as an encore with a kind of hair-raising unbridled virtuosity few such profound artists can command. No singer, either, has ever opened up the heavens as she did with those four recitatives in Handel's *Messiah* beginning with "There were shepherds abiding in the fields," and ending with: "And suddenly there was with the angels a multitude of the heavenly host ..."

And then, here is Jon Vickers as the *Otello* of our era—he who was also the *Parsifal*, the *Peter Grimes*, the Aeneas in *Les Troyens*: the only great tenor to scale with equal distinction these pinnacles of the Italian, the German, the English and the French repertoires. They talk about and assiduously televise "the three tenors". Vickers was four tenors in one. What leaps with particular vividness to my mind, though, is Vickers, senior alumnus of Toronto's Royal Conservatory, stepping slowly, quietly onto the platform at the conservatory's centennial gala, stopping time with sheer, unaffected presence and the power of silence before he began "Total Eclipse" from Handel's *Samson*. And then giving us the blinded Samson himself in that single aria.

The Curtin photograph of Maureen Forrester here reproduced reveals especially the honest young woman who has always lived in this most richly endowed of our great singers. Like the voices of Schumann-Heink and Anderson and Ferrier before her, Forrester's was a voice in a thousand, instantly recognizable and allied to an absolute generosity. Here is Forrester rehearsing a new work of R. Murray Schafer: without affectation, simply, betraying no shred of cynicism or conceit. This is the Forrester who delivered so stunningly those two Canadian masterpieces, Harry Somers' *Five Songs for Dark Voice* and Schafer's *Adieu, Robert Schumann*, both with the National Arts Centre Orchestra under Mario Bernardi. But this is the same Forrester who appeared at a final concert of the Canadian Music Competition Festival and gave the young performers and their parents and friends something to remember for the rest of their lives: a few songs containing in a nutshell the whole glamor, the undivided attention of the artist at work, the unstinting gift of a great performance from her to them.

In Curtin's photograph of Mario Bernardi I'm reminded of Stravinsky's remark that "technique is the whole man." Music is all, to this meticulous Canadian virtuoso of the baton who created the National Arts Centre Orchestra and recreated the Calgary Philharmonic and the CBC Vancouver Orchestra. Music invades and informs every cell of Bernardi's body and mind. Bach, Mozart, Berlioz, Schumann, Stravinsky; the French, the Canadians, of course the Italians; opera, symphony; our composers, our singers, our players, all have yielded up their secrets to this son of an Italian-immigrant Canadian blacksmith, who understands and coordinates with the fine, sure, classical touch of a Szell. Curtin's buoyant photo invokes a hundred performances with Bernardi quick at the helm: Mozart to melt the hardest heart, Berlioz to make your head spin, Tippett's *Fantasia concertante on a theme of Corelli* delving into the race memory of music in such a way as to ravish the senses and haunt the mind. No surprise at all was Bernardi's brilliant success in 1993 in London with Massenet's *Chérubin*, and you can see it foretold here.

And who could resist the serenely ecstatic moment Curtin has captured with that queen of organists Mireille Lagacé practising Bach; or the glorious shot of our burly baritone Louis Quilico in over his ample tummy and swimming for his life on the way to his memorable *Falstaff*; or the unforgettable glimpse of Metropolitan Opera soprano Teresa Stratas, here visibly moved on from the tiny tempestuous Toronto-Greek princess of our first memories to the consummate Verdian-Bergian-Brechtian actress of her *La Traviata* and *Lulu* and *Mahagonny*.

The pictures of the Orford Quartet are poignant, partly because the quartet is dispersed, and Canada's first purveyor of the whole quartet repertoire, including the substantial Canadian component from Pentland to Cherney, is now a memory and a handful of recordings. But for me, Curtin's pictures recapture not only this elegant ensemble's whole Beethoven and its Schafer *Waves*, but also its magical afternoons of Mendelssohn—the quartets and the quintets at Hart House. Poignant, too, is the photo of Elmer Iseler, conducting his marvellous choir of the '60s—the Festival Singers. That choir, with its singular pride of voices (Mary Morrison and Patricia Rideout were two of them), is now also dispersed, but it became a part of the larger history of music when Igor Stravinsky chose it for his own recording of his choral masterpiece, the *Symphony of Psalms*.

Composers are naturally the stiffest challenge for the Curtin camera. Their communicative activity has gone into their scores and they are less accustomed to baring their souls in their persons. Curtin knew he must be content to capture their numinosity for the most part through other means. Exceptions are: the photo of Schafer, our most eclectic and polemic master, who looks as if he's about to deliver one of the Shavian surprises that have peppered and salted his career; the photo of Eckhardt-Gramatté, volatile virtuoso (piano and violin) and composer, dropped in among us from Europe in 1953, and looking here on the verge of speaking her considerable mind; and the photo of Gabriel Charpentier, charming his way out of a corner with an actor's fluency. But when Curtin had to content himself with a composer's less overt numinosity he did so with the touch of a master. Here are: Weinzweig sprawled magisterially among the leaves of a score; Somers, patrician, rapt in his pages as Elmer Iseler and the Festival Singers rehearse them out of the frame; Beckwith nocturnally contemplating some sonic design by lamplight; Freedman dreaming his notes; Tremblay probing the piano for his; Morawetz interrupted at work; Colgrass, pensive as he hears his manuscript made sound; Anhalt in conference over the premiere of his *La Tourangelle*. These glimpses—so acutely chosen—remind us keenly of the musics of our time and place.

Needless to say, Curtin was still snapping when he sailed past his 80th birthday in 1991, so there's more to this small collection than nostalgia.

Not all the stars in our bright new constellation of singers made it in (no Donna Brown, no Gerald Finley, no Nancy Argenta, no Richard Margison), but I don't doubt Curtin has them in his files, ready for Collection No. 2. In the meantime, to represent them all, here are the imposing successors to Vickers and Forrester: Ben Heppner and Catherine Robbin. Heppner is the colossal young tenor (and first *McTeague*) whose Laca in the Metropolitan Opera's production of Janáček's *Jenůfa* was the thrill of 1992, and the range of whose roles must soon rival the range of Vickers'. Catherine Robbin is the poised, Toronto-born woman with the soundest, loveliest, most versatile mezzo-soprano since Janet Baker's. Here, too, is Russell Braun, a fledgling at this writing but what a fledgling! His Papageno in the Canadian Opera Company's *Magic Flute* was one of the most disarming I've ever heard.

Curtin has caught the current pianists at it, as well. In this collection we see Angela Hewitt, Arthur Ozolins, Monica Gaylord, and two—André Laplante and Louis Lortie—who are of particular interest because they represent at the highest level one of the great teachers of this era: the late Yvonne Hubert.

This extraordinary Montreal teacher produced not only Laplante and Lortie but a succession of career pianists (William Stevens, Ronald Turini, Janina Fialkowska, William Tritt, Marc-André Hamelin, Stéphane Lemelin), instilling in them all the French tradition of Marmontel through her own studies with Marguerite Long and Alfred Cortot. Each of Yvonne Hubert's young virtuosi has gone on to a maturity implicit in his or her gift, but each came from Hubert equipped with phenonenal skills and controls. I shall not soon forget coming across, in the CBC archives, the 15-year-old Louis Lortie's flabbergasting performance of Brahms' *Variations on a Theme of Handel*. Not since the revelations of the young Gould had I heard anything comparable. In Curtin's 1994 photograph Lortie is twice the age and his playing is commensurately wiser and deeper but still—and you can virtually *see* it here—flabbergasting.

Curtin's young fiddlers are all at the verge, save perhaps Peter Oundjian who is settled as first violin of the Tokyo Quartet. Curtin has caught Corey Cerovsek looking uncannily like Son of Steven Staryk, Martin Beaver beavering at his formidable technique quietly at home, and the questing Scott St-John, founder of the changeable chamber group Millenium, inciting someone to something.

We see these young string players with a surge of something like hope. The '80s and '90s have been troubled times in the arts, glum with cutbacks, retrenchments, philistine priorities, a slipping away of interest in aesthetic values. Yet here are these vigorous youths, asserting music afresh. In the words of Masefield:

> *'Lo, all my heart's field, red and torn,*
> *And Thou shalt bring the young, green corn;*
> *The young, green corn, divinely springing,*
> *The young, green corn, forever singing.'*

But enough. All of these photographs by Walter Curtin—the few here, the fewer I've mentioned, the many implied—catch Canada's aquarian age at precious moments of its specific fleeting reality. I long for them in wallsfull, like the paintings of Paul Klee.

*Glenn Gould at
Eaton Auditorium
recording session
11 February 1975,
seen in the National
Film Board's 1975
MusiCanada.*

*Glenn Gould in 196?
at his home on
St. Clair Avenue We?
in Toronto.*

*(Overleaf)
Glenn Gould in CBC
Studio, Jarvis St.,
2 February 1974.*

*(Previous spread) Glenn Gould and his dedicated colleague, the
sound engineer Lorne Tulk recording in Toronto's Eaton
Auditorium, 11 February 1975.*

Anton Kuerti at his home in Toronto, 14 September 1986.

**Arthur Ozolins rehears-
ing for a CBC concert
recording at Toronto's
Eaton Auditorium,
10 July 1974.**

*Ofra Harnoy and
James McKay
rehearsing at
Toronto's Royal
Conservatory of
Music in 1987.*

*Ofra Harnoy in her
home in Toronto, 26
November 1986.*

Harry Somers at a
rehearsal of the
Festival Singers in
Toronto's St. Anne's
Church on Gladstone
Avenue, 10 April
1976.

Oskar Morawetz in his Toronto home, 21 July 1974.

Wilfrid Pelletier conducting a youth ensemble at Toronto's Royal Conservatory of Music in 1971.

The Huggett family — Fiona, Jennifer, Leslie, Margaret and Andrew, rehearsing in their Uxbridge, Ontario home, 28 September 1981.

St.Lawrence Quartet:
Geoff Nuttal, Barry
Shiffman, Marina Hoover,
and Lesley Robertson.

(Overleaf) Zara Nelsova at rehearsal in Massey Hall for
a concert with the Toronto Symphony, 27 January 1975.

*The members of the Orford
String Quartet: Andrew
Dawes, Kenneth Perkins,
Denis Brott, and Terence
Helmer, at rehearsal in a
private Toronto home,
15 march 1985.*

John Weinzweig at his cottage at Kearney, Ontario, 28 August 1974.

(Top) Otto Joachim in his studio in Montreal, 8 October 1974.

Serge Garant conducting in the CBC studios in Montreal, 27 April 1978.

(Overleaf) Fujiko Imajishi warming up prior to a rehearsal for a CBC concert in Toronto's St. James' Cathedral, in the spring of 1973.

R. Murray Schafer at the
Faculty of Music, University of
Toronto, 27 October 1972.

Sonia Eckhardt-Gramatté,
22 June 1974.

(Previous spread)
Jon Washburn rehearsing for
a concert at the St. Lawrence
Centre in Toronto,
24 April 1980.

Mireille Lagacé practising at the Mount Orford, Quebec, summer music camp of Jeunesses musicales du Canada, 28 July 1975.

Lois McDonall in her dressing room at the English National Opera, London, preparing for her title role in Iain Hamilton's Anna Karenina, 22 May 1981.

Gino Quilico in his dressing room at the Paris Opera, 4 June 1984.

Ben Heppner rehearsing at Roy Thomson Hall in Toronto for International Choral Festival performance of Benjamin Britten's War Requiem, 6 June 1993.

Louis Applebaum at the rehearsal of the Masque of Comus *presented by COMUS Music Theatre at Toronto's Guild of All Arts, 10 June 1986.*

(Previous spread)
Gilles Tremblay working in his home in Montreal, 10 July 1974.

*John Beckwith in his
Toronto studio at his
home, 24 May 1974.*

*Harry Freedman con-
ducting a soundtrack
recording session at
the Toronto CBC
Yonge St. studios,
23 November 1973.*

*(Overleaf) Shauna Rolston in her dressing room at Toronto's Roy Thomson Hall, September 1989.
Tsuyoshi Tsutsumi rehearsing for a concert with The Chamber Players of Toronto in Walter Hall
at the Faculty of Music, 23 February 1973.*

Robert Aitken performing with The Chamber Players of Toronto in a Toronto CBC studio, for a television production, 1 April 1975.

(Previous spread) Canadian Brass members Graeme Page, Fred Mills, Ronald Romm, Charles Daellenback and Eugene Watts, with an unidentified dog, at the Banff Centre, Banff, Alberta, 21 July

*James Campbell per-
forming at the summer
Festival of the Sound,
Parry Sound, Ontario.*

Maureen Forrester rehearsing with the CJRT Orchestra in Toronto's Ryerson Theatre, Ryerson Polytechnical Institute, for a performance of a work by R. Murray Schafer, 14 October 1979.

(Overleaf) Elmer Iseler in rehearsal with the Festival Singers, in the Great Hall, Hart House, at the University of Toronto, 12 January 1973.

Roxolana Roslak in rehearsal at Toronto's Massey Hall, for a performance of Leonard Bernstein's Symphony No. 3 "Kaddish", in 1973.

*Jane Coop rehearsing
with The Toronto
Symphony in
Massey Hall,
27 March 1977.*

*(Overleaf) Gérard
Causse and Rivka Golani
performing in the
du Maurier Centre,
Harbourfront, Toronto
in 1987.*

71

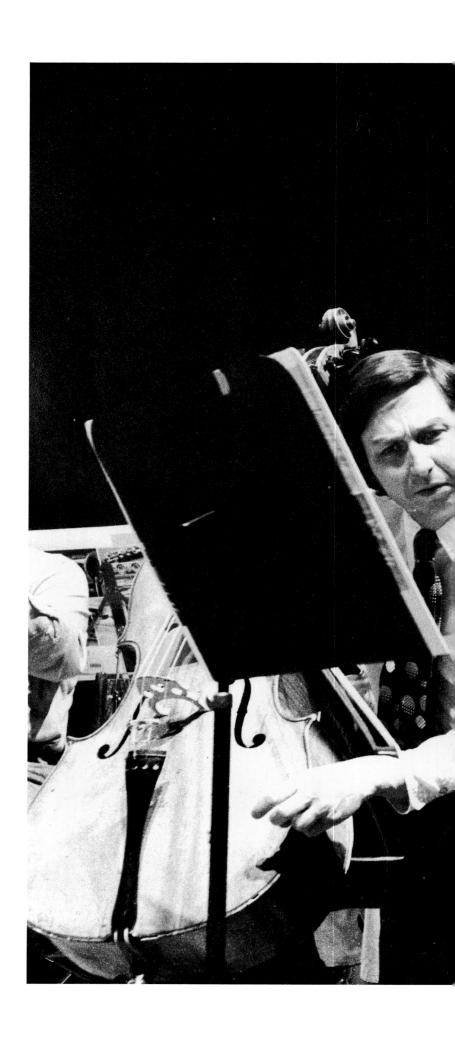

Ronald Laurie and Peter Schenkman in rehearsal with the CJRT Orchestra in the Ryerson Theatre, at Toronto's Ryerson Polytechnical Institute, 7 January 1978.

Marius Constant and István Anhalt with CBC technicians at a rehearsal for the premiere of Anhalt's La Tourangelle, *in the MacMillan Theatre, University of Toronto, July 1975.*

*Bernard Lagacé with
pupils at the Mount
Orford, Quebec summer
music camp of Jeunesses
musicales du Canada,
27 July 1975.*

Herman Geiger-Torel
directing a rehearsal
of the Canadian
Opera Company's
production of
Die Fledermaus *in the*
MacMillan Theatre,
University of
Toronto,
17 August 1975.

Edith Wiens in a dressing room
at Toronto's Roy Thomson Hall,
prior to a performance with
The Toronto Symphony,
14 September 1989.

(Overleaf) Jon Vickers, Roberta Knie and Maureen Forrester in the
Opéra du Québec's production of Wagner's Tristan und Isolde, *given at*
The Place des Arts, Montreal and televised by the CBC, 10 June 1975.

Victor Feldbrill
rehearsing the
University of
Toronto Symphony
Orchestra, in the
MacMillan Theatre,
20 October 1972.

Gabriel Charpentier at Jean Gascon's Montreal home, 5 October 1974.

Louis Quilico and director Carlo Maestrini in rehearsal for the Opéra du Québec's production of Falstaff *at the Montreal Place des Arts, 3 October 1974.*

*Michael Colgrass at
a rehearsal of the
National Arts Centre
Orchestra in Ottawa,
for the premiere of
his composition Delta
in 1979.*

*Neil Chotem in rehearsal with James De Preist and
the Quebec Symphony Orchestra, for performances of
Chotem's composition Rhapsodie Québécoise on the
orchestra's 1980 northern Quebec Tour.*

*(Previous spread) Barbara Carter, Émile Belcourt, Judith Forst and Paul Frey in rehearsal at the University
of Toronto's Faculty of Music, for the 1976 Guelph Spring Festival production of Benjamin Britten's* Beggar's Opera.

(Overleaf) Andrew Davis rehearsing The Toronto Symphony *in Massey Hall, during his first season as
music director, 3 May 1976.*

(Left) Guy Lachapelle of the Montreal Symphony Orchestra in Place des Arts, during the filming of a section in The Music of Man television series by the CBC, 22 June 1978. (Other percussionist is unidentified)

(Overleaf) Teresa Stratas in her New York home, as she was being interviewed by Ulla Colgrass for Music Magazine, 29 November 1979.

*Lois Marshall rehearsing
in Walter Hall, Faculty of
Music, University of
Toronto, 11 January 1973.*

Lotfi Mansouri directing a rehearsal for the Canadian Opera Company's production of Britten's Peter Grimes, *12 April 1980.*

(Opposite)
Corey Cerovsek
photographed in the
studio of Isabel Kann,
29 April 1994.

(Top left)
Martin Beaver in his
Toronto home,
16 May 1994.

(Top right)
Scott St. John at the
Festival of the Sound,
Parry Sound,
Ontario.

Peter Oundjian of the
Tokyo String Quartet
at the St. Lawrence
Centre, Toronto, 15
May 1993.

Louis Lortie rehearsing in the Glenn Gould Studio, at the Toronto CBC building, 26 April 1994.

*Norbert Kraft at the
Sharon Temple, Sharon,
Ontario, during the summer
concert series Music at
Sharon, 5 July 1986.*

*Liona Boyd photographed
in Toronto,
5 January 1983.*

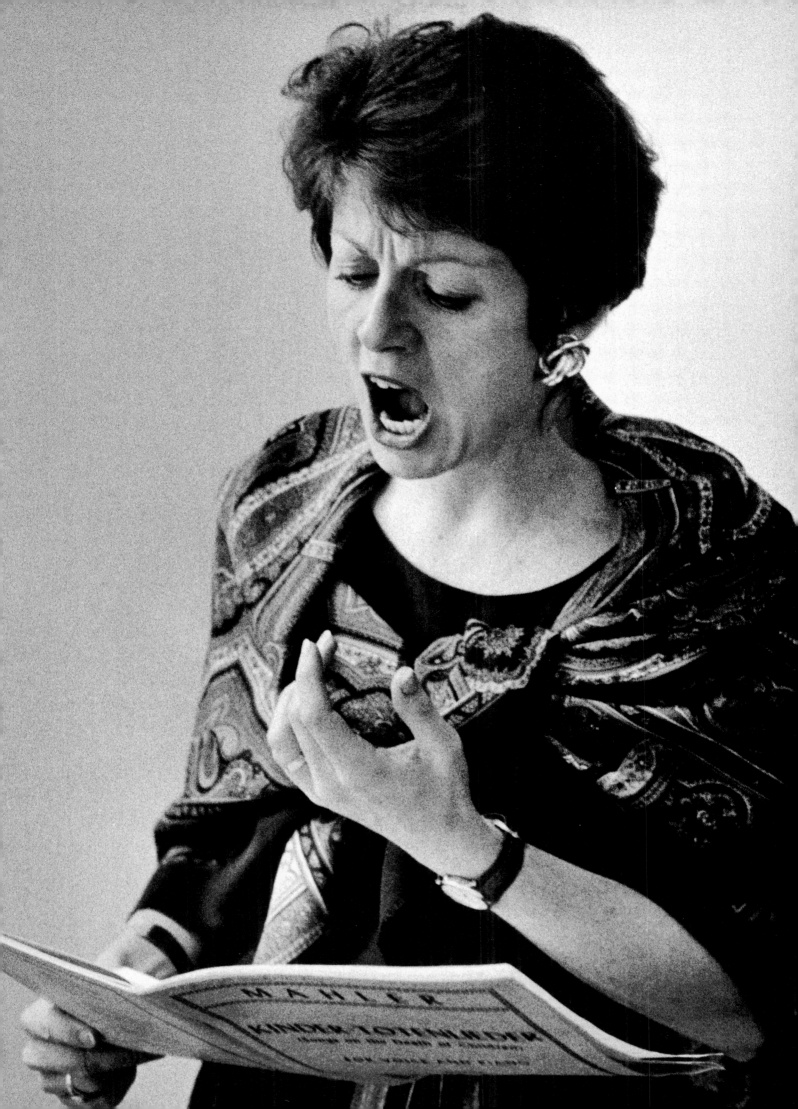

*Frances Marr and
Harry Adaskin in their
Vancouver home,
23 July 1978.*

*Alexina Louie at the
Faculty of Music,
University of Toronto.*

*(Previous spread) Left: Russell Braun and Carolyn Maule at their home, Thornhill, Ontario,
16 October 1992. Right: Catherine Robbin in Isabel Kann's studio, 12 May 1994.*

*(Overleaf) Karel Ančerl at Massey Hall, in rehearsal with cellist Vladimir Orloff and
The Toronto Symphony, April 1973.*

*Antonín Kubálek rehearsing for a
CBC concert at Toronto's Eaton
Auditorium, 7 November 1974.*

*André Laplante in Kingston,
Ontario at Queen's University,
24 October 1979.*

*Angela Hewitt in War Memorial
Hall, preparing for her appearance
at the Guelph Spring Festival,
Guelph, Ontario, 14 May 1985.*

*Monica Gaylord
performing at a
New Music Concert
series in Walter
Hall, University of
Toronto,
1 December 1973.*

Monica Gaylord and Heléna Bowkun (who is resting on the floor of the Art Gallery of Ontario's Walker court) rehearsing for a CBC concert perfor-mance of James Montgomery's Riverrun, *composed for three amplified pianos, 6 April 1978.*

*Mario Bernardi rehearsing
in Ottawa's National
Arts Centre*

Jukka-Pekka Saraste,
Fall 1994

Tafelmusik's Jean Lamon,
1994

The Musicians

by Patricia Wardrop

Adaskin, Harry OC

Harry Adaskin, violinist, teacher and broadcaster, was born in Latvia in 1901, but was brought to Toronto as an infant. He studied violin at several of the city's music schools. He played in local theater orchestras and chamber ensembles before becoming the original second violinist of the Hart House String Quartet in 1923, a position he held until 1938. This group—arguably the best-known Canadian chamber ensemble of its time, toured extensively in Canada and the United States, and also in Europe; it was heard often on radio. Adaskin and his wife, the pianist Frances Marr, formed a duo which devoted many of its recitals to contemporary and commissioned compositions. Adaskin began his long association with CBC radio in 1938 when he started his lecture series "Musically Speaking" and he continued to act as a host-raconteur well into the 1970s. Invited to establish music courses at the University of British Columbia, Adaskin moved to Vancouver in 1946. He taught until 1973, then published his memoirs in two volumes. Adaskin died in Vancouver in 1994.

Aitken, Robert CM

Aitken's career has been as varied as his many talents. He is a flutist, a composer and a teacher. Born in Nova Scotia in 1939, he studied flute and composition, earning a degree from the University of Toronto in 1961. He has performed as an orchestral musician, as a member of several chamber ensembles—including the Lyric Arts Trio—and has received truly international recognition as a soloist and recording artist in the Far East, North and Central America and in Europe. He is in demand for his performances of technically taxing contemporary music. His list of compositions includes works for orchestra, chamber groups, and electronic media. An active proponent of twentieth-century music, Aitken was a co-founder in 1971 of Toronto's successful New Music Concerts, has been its artistic director since the series' outset, and often conducted its programmes. In addition, he has given much of his time to teaching and master classes, both at centers throughout Canada, in Europe and in the United States.

Anhalt, István

Born in 1919, Anhalt studied with Zoltán Kodály in his native Hungary. After the war he resumed his piano and composition studies in Paris until he was able to emigrate to Canada in 1949, where he joined the music faculty at McGill to teach composition and theory. His beneficial influence on a generation of music students was widened when he moved to Kingston, Ontario in 1971, to head the Music Department at Queen's University. During his years at McGill he became interested in and became active in the creation and performance of electronic music. His compositions—some large-scale stage works such as *La Tourangelle* and *Winthrop*—reveal Anhalt's ability to integrate the traditional musical forms with the newer vocal and electronic techniques, to create a richly textured sonic tapestry. He has written extensively about music and is the author of the librettos for several of his compositions.

Ančerl, Karel

Karel Ančerl succeeded Seiji Ozawa as conductor and music director of the Toronto Symphony in 1969. During the four years in which he determined the the musical quality of the orchestra, he won the admiration of its musicians and its audience alike, for the depth and wealth of his musical ideas and his ability to communicate them. Born in Bohemia in 1908, Ančerl received his rigorous and thorough music training in Prague, and had embarked on a conducting career when, in 1939, the Nazis imprisoned him in a concentration camp. He alone, of all his family, survived the war. He began his personal life again, and returned to his beloved music. By 1951 he was the music director of the Czech Philharmonic. He was active on the international scene as well. Ančerl was guest conducting in the USA when the Russians invaded Czechoslovakia in 1968. Once again, his life was forced to take a new direction, one which brought him and his family as residents of Toronto. His untimely death in 1973 deprived the community and the world of a man of great musical stature and intelligence.

Applebaum, Louis OC

Toronto-born Louis Applebaum has enjoyed a long, distinguished career as composer, conductor and administrator. In the last-named capacity he has made a notable contribution to music in Canada, and to the development of Canadian culture in its broadest sense, through his work with CAPAC (Composers, Authors and Publishers Association of Canada), as former director of the Ontario Arts Council, and as chair of the 1980 Federal Cultural Policy Review Committee. However, music composition has always remained an integral part of his busy life. Applebaum began his career by preparing (and often conducting) hundreds of film scores for Canada's National Film Board and for studios in Hollywood. He has written incidental music for theater, radio and television, and has created ballet scores. His foyer fanfares, composed for the first Stratford production in 1953, continue to summon audiences forty years later. Applebaum's many commissions include music for orchestra, choirs, bands and for chamber ensembles.

Beaver, Martin

Martin Beaver was born in Winnepeg, grew up in Hamilton, Ontario, and started playing the violin as a small child. He studied at Toronto's Royal Conservatory with Victor Danchenko, then went on to earn his Artist's Diploma at Indiana University, where he worked with Josef Gingold. He has won a number of major awards—a silver medal at Belgium's 1993 Queen Elisabeth Competition—and he was the recipient of the Canada Council's prestigious Virginia P. Moore award that same year. He is a favorite performer at music festivals in Canada and abroad, has performed in a duo with pianist Jamie Parker, given many recitals and appeared as guest soloist with a number of orchestras, Mr. Beaver returned to the Royal Conservatory in 1990—this time as a member of the teaching faculty.

Beckwith, John CM

John Beckwith exemplifies the versatility that is needed to survive as a Canadian composer. Long committed to the development of a national musical voice, he has devoted his talents—and they are considerable—not only to the composition of music in many genres (operas and stage works, chamber and instrumental pieces, choral and orchestral works), but also has been an outstanding teacher, a broadcaster, music critic, programme annotator, writer, editor, administrator and board member. Beckwith's contribution to the *Encyclopedia of Music in Canada* and to the Canadian Musical Heritage Society helped ensure the success of both projects. Born and raised in Victoria, B.C., he has spent most of his professional life in Toronto. Beckwith, now retired from the Faculty of Music at the University of Toronto, continues to be a persuasive advocate for Canada's creative musical community, and of course, he continues to compose.

Belcourt, Émile

Émile Belcourt is a character tenor with a wide range of roles in his repertoire. He was born near Regina, Saskatchewan in 1926, and in the early 1950's studied music in Vienna. Although he has sung on occasion with the Canadian Opera Company, the Edmonton Opera and at the Guelph Spring Festival, the greater part of his musical career has been spent in England, where he is a member of the English National Opera (formerly known as the Sadler's Wells). Belcourt also appeared to great critical acclaim in the Seattle Opera's Pacific Northwest Wagner Festival for five seasons, during which he performed the roles of Loge, Siegmund and Tristan.

Bernardi, Mario CC

Of Italian heritage, Mario Bernardi was born in Kirkland Lake, Ontario in 1930, received his early music education in Venice, then completed his studies at Toronto's Royal Conservatory of Music. He established his reputation as a pianist and accompanyist before embarking on what has been an outstanding career as a conductor — one who has served the orchestral and operatic musical life in his country, and abroad, with great distinction. He was the founding music director of the National Arts Centre Orchestra in Ottawa in 1969, and during his thirteen-year tenure developed a virtuoso ensemble that became internationally known because of its tours and recordings. He was the musical director of Ottawa's successful Summer Opera Festival, and has conducted at leading opera houses throughout North America and in Europe. Bernardi has led all of Canada's major orchestras, recorded with many, and at present is Principal Conductor Laureate of the Calgary Philharmonic where he was music director from 1984. Bernardi makes his home in Toronto.

Boulanger, Nadia

This renowned French teacher, composer and conductor had an extraordinary influence on the development of music and musical life in Canada. Between 1920 and her death in 1979 (she was born in 1887), countless numbers of young Canadian pupils and would-be musicians flocked to her studio in Paris, to submit themselves to the rigors of her classes in harmony, counterpoint and analysis; and to her demands for accuracy, taste, and clear and logical expression in form. Boulanger imbued her pupils with a high sense of discipline and of the standards that must be achieved for the proper creation or performance of any composition.

Bowkun, Heléna

Pianist Heléna Bowkun was born in Toronto and studied piano at the Royal Conservatory of Music and at the University of Toronto. Her teachers included Pierre Souvairan and Leon Fleisher. Bowkun is an admired solo performer and recitalist, and she has performed and recorded with such musicians as violinist Steven Staryk, flutist Robert Aitken and cellist Ofra Harnoy. Bowkun's repertoire is broad in scope. She has achieved an enviable mastery of technically challenging compositions of all periods. As a teacher, adjudicator and writer, she is committed to the all-round education of young musicians.

Boyd, Liona CM

Although born in London, England, guitarist Liona Boyd received her early musical training in Toronto with Eli Kassner, after her family settled in that city. Boyd later studied with, among others, Alexandre Lagoya in Paris. She made her New York debut in 1975, and began a series of performance tours that have taken her throughout North America and countries around the globe. Her numerous recordings and TV appearances have ensured this popular artist a wide audience and she has responded by programming music of a diverse nature—from baroque to rock, classical to country. Boyd also composes and transcribes music for her instrument, and has published several volumes of these works.

Braun, Russell

The son of the well-known Canadian baritone Victor Braun, Russell Braun was born in Frankfurt, Germany in 1965, and is, like his father, possessed of an exceptional baritone voice. Since his graduation from the Opera Division at the University of Toronto, where he studied with Patricia Kern, he has appeared with the Canadian Opera Company, Opera Hamilton, the New York City Opera, Pacific Opera and the Vancouver Opera; has performed as a guest soloist with a number orchestras, and has taken part in summer festival programmes at Elora and Sharon, and at the Festival of the Sound.

Campbell, James

Clarinetist James Campbell has enjoyed an international concert career, appearing with orchestras, chamber ensembles, and in recital throughout Canada, the United States, in Europe, Asia, Australia and South America. This Alberta native, who studied in both Canada and the United States, and was the winner of several important competitions, has made many recordings that display his ability to perform music in a wide range of styles and periods. Campbell became the artistic director of the annual summer Festival of the Sound (at Parry Sound, Ontario) in 1985, and has further developed its popular appeal with an interesting and eclectic mix of programming. He also finds time, in his busy performing schedule, to teach at Indiana University, where he is a professor at the Music School.

Canadian Brass

Canadian Brass has earned a large and loyal following since the group began performing in 1970. Its lively, informal style, underscored by the discipline and technical excellence of the members, plus the broad range of its repertoire, all has great appeal to the world-wide audiences who have enjoyed its concert tours. Hornist Graeme Page (born in Toronto), trombonist Eugene Watts (born in Missouri), and tubist Charles Daellenbach (from Wisconsin), were founding members, and were joined by trumpeters Ronald Romm (from New York) in 1971, and by Fred Mills (from Guelph, Ontario) in 1972. The group's members were artists-in-residence with the Hamilton Philharmonic Orchestra 1971-1977. Canadian Brass has commissioned and premiered a number of works by Canadian composers, has issued dozens of recordings, and has made appearances with orchestras in concert, been seen on film and on television. They reached a new audience when the members joined the gang on "Sesame Street" and "The Muppet Show".

Carter, Barbara

A coloratura soprano, Barbara Carter studied at the Opera School of the University of Toronto. She has sung supporting and leading roles in productions with the Canadian Opera Company, Opera in Concert, the Guelph Spring Festival, Festival Ottawa and the Stratford Festival. She moved to Germany in 1978 and has sung as a company member with Deutscher Oper Berlin.

Causse, Gérard

A French violist, Gérard Causse participated, together with Rivka Golani, in the 1987 premiere of *Viola Duet*, composed by Canadian Bruce Mather. This was part of a New Music Concerts programme.

Cerovsek, Corey

The prodigious talent of the young violinist, born in Vancouver in 1972, earned him a place in the music school at Indiana University when he was only twelve years old—the youngest student ever to enrol there. He studied with Josef Gingold. By 1991 Cerovsek had received graduate degrees at both the master and doctoral levels. He has performed throughout Canada and the United States, both with orchestras and also in recital, and made his European debut in 1987 in London.

Charpentier, Gabriel

A composer and poet, Gabriel Charpentier has expressed his life-long and deeply-felt commitment to the performing arts in a variety of ways. He has composed operas and musical theater pieces, written librettos for his and other composers' works, and has prepared the music for dozens of theatrical productions, including seventeen for the Stratford Festival. He has acted as an artistic adviser and programmer for Montreal's CBC-TV, and was a co-founder of COMUS Music Theater in Toronto. He has taught at the National Theatre School and at McGill University. Born and educated in Quebec (later in Paris), Charpentier's early interest in, and study of, Georgian chant with the Benedictines at St-Benoît-du-Lac, was to be a basic and recurring element particularly in his vocal and theatrical works. In addition his use of counterpoint and complex rhythmic details enriches his music in whatever form.

Chotem, Neil

Born in Saskatoon in 1920, the classically trained pianist Neil Chotem settled in Montreal following his war service in the RCAF. His professional activities as performer, composer, arranger, conductor and teacher, reveal his wide-ranging musical interests and the diversity of his talents. He has led a jazz trio, taught orchestration and arranging, performed concertos with Canadian orchestras and on CBC radio, composed music for a number of CBC radio plays and series, and has made arrangements for pop performers including Michel Rivard, Rénee Claude, and Harmonium. Chotem has conducted Canadian orchestras in live concerts and for recording sessions. This versatile musician resists labels and defies categorization.

Colgrass, Michael

Michael Colgrass, a native of Chicago, received his training as a percussionist and a composer in the United States. He settled in Toronto in 1974. Colgrass has received commissions from orchestras and festivals on both sides of the forty-ninth parallel. Many of his compositions have been published and a number have been recorded. One work—*Déja vu*—won a 1978 Pulitzer Prize; another—*Strangers: Irreconcilable Variations for Clarinet, Viola and Piano*—was awarded the Jules Léger Prize for New Chamber Music in 1988.

Constant, Marius

This Rumanian-born French conductor and composer has had a long association with Canadian music and musicians. He visited Canada to act as a juror for CBC talent competitions, and for four seasons was the conductor of the National Youth Orchestra. Because of his strong personal interest in twentieth-century music, and his particular interest of multi-media works, he has been the guest conductor for a number of Canadian premieres, including that of István Anhalt's *La Tourangelle* in 1975 in Toronto. Constant was one of the conductors at the inaugural concert of the Canadian Cultural Center in Paris in 1970.

Coop, Jane

The career of pianist Jane Coop has taken her literally across Canada. She was born in Saint John in 1950, grew up in Calgary and studied there and in Toronto, before taking advanced training in Europe and the United States. In addition to an international concert and recital performance schedule, she has maintained an active teaching career, working as an assistant to Anton Kuerti at the University of Toronto, before joining the faculty at the University of British Columbia in 1980, in Vancouver, where she now lives. She is in demand as an accompanist and as a chamber musician. Coop has issued a number of recordings that cover a broad spectrum of the piano literature, and these display her appealing and sensitive musicianship and superb technical command of her chosen instrument.

Davis, Andrew

Andrew Davis was appointed music director of the Toronto Symphony in 1975 at the age of thirty-one. Born in England, he had studied piano and gained a music degree from Cambridge where he had been Organ Scholar. He studied conducting with Franco Ferrara in Rome, then embarked on a career that included both concert and opera engagements in the British Isles and the United States. During his thirteen years with the Toronto Symphony he expanded its repertoire, led the orchestra on several of its national and international tours, and made a number of recordings. Following his return to England he was named Director of the Glyndbourne Festival Opera and Music Director of the BBC Symphony in London.

As Conductor Laureate, he returns frequently to lead the Toronto Symphony Orchestra.

De Preist, James

A nephew of the illustrious contralto, Marian Anderson, James De Preist was born in Philadelphia and studied at the University of Pennsylvania. He had been assistant conductor of the New York Philharmonic, then the National Symphony Orchestra in Washington before his appointment in 1975 as leader of the Quebec Symphony Orchestra. He helped to guide Canada's oldest orchestra to a new level of excellence, and included the performance of contemporary works—many commissioned from Canadian composers—during the organization's celebratory seventy-fifth season in 1977-8. De Preist remained Music Director until 1983 when he returned to the United States to continue his career.

Eckhardt-Gramatté, SC

The extraordinary public music career of Russian-born Sophie-Carmen (Sonia) began when a prodigious eleven-year-old gave solo concerts on both the piano and the violin. However, her abiding musical interest was in composition, but it was not until 1930 (when she was 31) that she determined to give up performance and become a composer. By the late 1940's her works were receiving international recognition and awards. She moved to Winnipeg in 1953 because her husband, Ferdinand Eckhardt, became director of the Art Gallery there. She continued an active and influential musical life in her adopted country, that included composition (for orchestra, for chamber ensembles, for piano), and teaching. Eckhardt-Gramatté held strong and highly personal opinions about teaching methods for both piano and violin. She died in 1974 during a visit to Europe. Her wish to encourage young musicians to play the music of their contemporaries was realized with the establishment in 1976 of an eponymous instrumental/vocal competition held annually in Brandon, Manitoba.

Feldbrill, Victor OC

When Sir Ernest MacMillan asked an eighteen-year-old Toronto violinist to conduct the Toronto Symphony Orchestra during a Student Concert in 1943, he re-routed Victor Feldbrill's musical career. Feldbrill has since conducted every major orchestra in Canada, including CBC radio and television ensembles, as well as opera orchestras such as the Canadian Opera Company. He was the music director of the Winnipeg Symphony and of the Hamilton Philharmonic, and he has had a long association with orchestras in Japan. In addition he has conducted in China, Russia and the Philippines. Long a champion of contemporary Canadian composition, Feldbrill has premiered and more importantly re-programmed the orchestral and operatic works of over two dozen

Canadian composers. His commitment to the training of young musicians has involved him as a staff member of the Faculty of Music, University of Toronto for fourteen years; in a special relationship with the National Youth Orchestra, and with the Youth Orchestra of the Toronto Symphony, which he helped establish.

Forrester, Maureen CC
This world-famous contralto has enjoyed a long and varied career as a performer, a teacher and an administrator. Born and raised in Montreal, Forrester made her professional debut there in 1951, a European debut in 1955, and gave her first recital in New York city in 1956. She has performed on five continents, either in recital, as a soloist with major conductors and orchestras in oratorios and concerts, and as a member of the Bach Aria Group. Her extensive discography indicates the scope and diversity of her repertoire. She has been a champion of the vocal music of Canadian composers and has premiered a number of their works. Forrester began to give master classes in the mid-1960s, and has taught in both Canada and the United States. In addition to her volunteer administrative positions, Forrester was the Chairman of the Canada Council from 1983 to 1988. She has received many honors and awards for her devotion to the musical life and cultural health of Canada.

Forst, Judith OC
Because of her outstanding performance at the Metropolitan Opera Auditions, Judith Forst was offered a contract and made her debut there in 1968. She was a member of the company and lived in New York until 1975. Forst was born in New Westminster, B.C. in 1943, and had studied music at the University of British Columbia and been part of the Vancouver Opera training programme. A mezzo-soprano with a bright, clear coloratura flexibility, she has sung with opera companies throughout Canada and the United States in parts that display the dramatic capability of her voice, her vocal security and her emotional intensity: *Cenerentola*, Marie in *Wozzeck*, the Composer in *Ariadne auf Naxos*, Kostelnicka in *Jenůfa*. Judith Forst lives in Port Moody, B.C.

Freedman, Harry OC
Two early interests have continued to influence the music of this Polish-born, Canadian-educated composer: painting and jazz. Freedman first studied clarinet in Winnipeg, but following wartime service in the RCAF, he settled in Toronto and studied oboe and composition at the Conservatory of Music. He joined the Toronto Symphony Orchestra as English horn in 1946 and remained a member for twenty-five years, after which he devoted all his time to composition. His long list of works includes a number of ballet scores, incidental music for theater, television and many films (*Act of the Heart, The Pyx*), orchestral and chamber music, and music for voice—both solo and choral—for which he often supplies the texts.

Some of Freedman's compositions have been inspired by specific Canadian painters and paintings, but the color, form and vision of an artist is never absent from any of his work. He has taught both orchestration and composition and has been an active lobbyist on behalf of Canadian composers.

Frey, Paul
Born in Heidelberg, Ontario and of Mennonite background, Paul Frey sang in Kitchener's Schneider Male Chorus, whose director, Paul Berg, encouraged the young man to take vocal lessons. He enroled at the Opera School of the University of Toronto in the mid-1970s, where he worked with Louis Quilico. However, it was not until his move to Europe in 1978 and his subsequent engagement at the Stadttheater Basel that his career as a lyric Heldentenor of international repute began to truly blossom. By 1987 he was singing lead Wagnerian roles at Bayreuth and other major European opera houses, including Covent Garden. Frey made his Metropolitan Opera debut in 1987 as Bacchus in *Ariadne auf Naxos*, and has since appeared with opera companies in the United States, and Australia and with leading orchestras in North America. Frey's performances in *Fidelio* and *Der Freischütz* have received particular acclaim from critics and audiences.

Garant, Serge OC
It is difficult to describe, let alone summarize, the role and varied contribution of this Quebec composer, conductor, pianist, teacher and critic, to the contemporary music scene in Canada. He was born in Quebec City in 1929, first was a jazz musician on clarinet and saxophone; then he studied composition and piano in Montreal and Paris, where he turned decisively in the direction of the avant-garde. His compostional, conducting and teaching energies were focused on the music and techniques of the twentieth-century, and all his work earned an enthusiastic following from the public as well as his pupils and his fellow composers. Garant was one of the founders, and for twenty years the artistic director, of the Société de musique contemporaine du Québec (SMCQ), and also conductor of its performance ensemble. This organization gave concerts, toured in Canada and Europe, and premiered countless new compositions. Garant had been much honored for his work before his untimely death in Sherbrooke, Quebec in 1986.

Gaylord, Monica
Toronto-based pianist Monica Gaylord was born in New York city and studied at the Juilliard School. She moved to Canada in 1970 and has been the orchestral pianist with both the Toronto Symphony and the National Arts Centre Orchestra in Ottawa. Gaylord has appeared as a guest soloist with a number of Canadian orchestras, and has also performed with various chamber ensembles including some of the New Music

Concerts series. She has made a number of recordings both as an accompanyist and as a soloist. Respected for her judgement, she has acted as juror and as an adjudicator. She became a member of the staff of Toronto's Royal Conservatory in 1986, where, in addition to teaching duties, she has contributed to piano publications.

Geiger-Torel, Herman OC

Herman Geiger-Torel was a pivotal figure in the development of opera performance in Canada. Born in Germany in 1907, he had a long association as a stage director in several Latin American countries before coming to Toronto in 1948, at the invitation of Nicholas Goldschmidt, to work at the newly-established Royal Conservatory Opera School. Until his retirement in 1976 from his position as General Director, he oversaw the artistic growth of what became the Canadian Opera Company, using a combination of shrewd administrative powers, keen musicianship, and a thorough knowledge of all aspects of stage and opera technique. He was also the stage director of numerous productions for other opera companies in Canada, the United States, and for CBC-TV. He maintained his association with the University's Opera School, and following his sudden death in 1976, the rehearsal room in the faculty's Opera Division was named in his memory.

Golani, Rivka

Rivka Golani is one of the outstanding violists performing today. Her magnetic and compelling stage presence, her technical mastery of her instrument, and her intense powers of musical communication have earned her high praise in the international musical community. Born in Tel Aviv where she studied, she moved to Canada in 1974. In addition to the traditional concert repertoire for viola, Golani has premiered well over one hundred works by more than forty composers, most written for her. She is in the process of recording all the major viola compositions. She is, as well, a visual artist, who has exhibited her paintings and published a book of her drawings. Highly respected as a teacher, many of her pupils at the University of Toronto have gone on to careers as professional musicians.

Gould, Glenn

When Glenn Gould died in his native Toronto in 1982, at the age of fifty, it was front-page news around the world. Despite the fact that this unique pianist had ceased to perform as a concert artist in 1964—he had made his recital debut in 1947—his recordings, writings, compositions, and radio and television documentaries had gained him an ever-increasing and devoted audience. He is regarded by some (in spite of his very selective repertoire) as one of the greatest pianists of the twentieth century; by others as a communications visionary who pushed the bounds of recording technology beyond its perceived limits; and by still others as a philosopher-aesthetician.

He, and his ideas, had detractors, often musicians, who rejected his personal approach to performance on whatever media. Since his death, all of Gould's recordings have been or are being re-issued, his writings collected, compiled and republished. There have been exhibitions, conferences and colloquia devoted to him. His films and TV programs have been made available; a recent feature film presents thirty-two snapshots of his life, and the Glenn Gould Society (founded in the Netherlands in 1982) sponsors events and publishes a biannual *Bulletin* of essays and writings. Gould centered his life and work in Toronto, where he could maintain the personal privacy that was so necessary to him. He used technology to communicate to others through time and space, and this continues to allow us to approach his art and genius.

Harnoy, Offra

An extensive list of recordings, many appearances as a guest soloist with orchestras in Canada, the United States, Europe, Israel, Australia and Japan, plus a handful of major music prizes and awards, belie the actual years of this young cellist. Offra Harnoy was born in Israel in 1965, moved to Toronto in 1971, and studied in that city and then in England. She began performing publicly before she reached her teens, but she has moved with ease from the role of child prodigy to that of a mature performer who has been selected to premiere new or recently discovered cello concertos. The depth of her musicianship and her dedication to the music of her chosen instrument have gained her both critical and public acclaim.

Heppner, Ben

Ben Heppner was born in Murrayville, in British Columbia's lower Fraser Valley. He studied at the University of British Columbia, won the 1979 CBC Talent Festival, then worked at the University of Toronto Opera Division. He gained international recognition when he was honored at the Metropolitan Opera Auditions with the Birgit Nilsson Prize. He has since earned an enviable reputation in his performances in major European and American opera houses, and has been chosen to sing in the world premieres of operas by Harry Somers and William Bolcolm. In demand as well in the concert hall, Heppner has appeared with orchestras in Canada and the United States. He has made recordings with such conductors as James Levine, Colin Davis and Wolfgang Sawallish. His powerful and dramatic tenor voice is particularly suited to the roles of Florestan, Peter Grimes, Lohengrin, and Walther von Stolzing.

Hewitt, Angela

Angela Hewitt grew up in a musical family. Her father is the Ottawa organist Godfrey Hewitt; her mother, Marion, was Angela's first piano teacher. She took her advanced studies in Toronto, at the University of Ottawa, and in France. As a young pianist she won major awards at a number of international competitions, but when she emerged as the winner of the 1985 International Bach Piano Competition in Toronto, she received the kind of practical rewards—scheduled concerts, the guaranteed release of a recital recording—which truly launched her career. As a guest soloist she has appeared with orchestras in Europe, Canada, Japan, and the United States, and she has given recitals as well. Known for her affinity with the music of Bach, her interpretation of the music of Schumann and Ravel has, as well, drawn appreciative praise. At present Hewitt makes her home in London, England, but often returns to Canada to perform.

The Huggett Family
This family musical performance group—Leslie and Margaret and their four children, Andrew, Jennifer, Ian and Fiona—were originally based in Ottawa, where they began their professional career in 1969, as a vocal and instrumental ensemble devoted to the music and dance of the medieval, renaissance and baroque periods. All sang, and together they played thirty-two different instruments, including woodwinds and strings. Their concerts were developed around specific themes, and they wore costumes of the period. The Huggett family performed throughout Canada, appeared at festivals, were included in films and television, and made a number of recordings before they disbanded in 1982 to pursue their individual careers.

Imajishi, Fujiko
Fujiko Imajishi enjoys the busy life of a highly skilled and versatile ensemble player and chamber musician. She was born in Tokyo, and studied violin, graduating from the Toho Music University. She chose to travel to Toronto in 1969 in order to study with the well-known violin teacher, Lorand Fenyves, at the University of Toronto. She received her degree in 1972, and for four years was a member of the Toronto Symphony. Imajishi has been concertmaster of the National Ballet of Canada orchestra, and holds that position in the Esprit Orchestra. She performs with many other groups and ensembles in the city. She is a member of the prestigious Saito Kinen Orchestra, conducted by Seiji Ozawa—an orchestra formed of Toho graduates who gather once a year to rehearse, tour (often in Europe), and take part in concerts in Japan.

Iseler, Elmer OC
A native of Port Colborne, Ontario, Elmer Iseler studied music at the University of Toronto, graduating with a degree in music education in 1950. He had joined the Toronto Mendelssohn Choir as a tenor in 1947, and in the early 1950's while a school music teacher, he founded and conducted the Festival Singers, a chamber choir that quickly became known for the excellence of its interpretation of the choral repertoire, but particularly of contemporary music. It was Canada's first fully professional choir. When Iseler was named the

sixth conductor of the Toronto Mendelssohn Choir, he became Canada's first full-time choral conductor. He has introduced audiences to new and little-known choral repertoire; he has toured Europe, Canada and the Far East with his group, The Elmer Iseler Singers (which he established in 1979), and he has been an honored specialist at symposia, conferences and workshops wherever and whenever choral musicians gather together.

Joachim, Otto
Joachim, who has centered his Canadian musical life in Montreal, was born into a musical family in Germany in 1910. He studied violin and viola. He emigrated to Canada (via China) in 1949, joined the Montreal Symphony Orchestra as well as other chamber ensembles. Because of his keen interest in early music and its instruments, he was a founder in 1958, and directed, the Montreal Consort of Ancient Instruments. He taught at McGill. However, it is composition that has dominated his creative life—particularly composition using the techniques and technology of the twentieth century. As early as the mid-1950s he set up a private electronic music studio, and assisted in the establishment of such a facility at McGill. It was Joachim who created the 4-track tape *Katimavik* for the Canada Pavillion at Expo 67—music heard by hundreds of thousands of visitors. His non-electronic compositions employ serial techniques and he is admired for his ability to use aleatoric or chance elements in his compositions.

Knie, Roberta
Roberta Knie was born in Oklahoma. A soprano of international reputation, she made her first Canadian appearance in the 1975 production of *Tristan and Isolde* in Montreal. This was the last opera to be presented by the Opèra du Québec.

Kraft, Norbert
A classical guitarist of international repute, Kraft was born in Austria but was brought to Toronto as a child. Before taking formal studies with Carl van Feggelen, then Eli Kassner, he played electric guitar in rock groups. Kraft has played throughout Canada, in the United States, Europe, and Asia, as guest soloist with orchestras, as a recitalist, and in a duo with his wife, the harpsichordist Bonnie Silver. Kraft has had a number of contemporary works commissioned for him, and he himself has composed, arranged and transcribed music for the guitar. He is the compiler and editor of a series of graded classical guitar music for students. He may be heard on a number of recordings, and appears often on radio and television. Kraft teaches at the University of Toronto and at the Royal Conservatory of Music.

Kubálek, Antonín
In 1968 Antonín Kubálek decided to leave his native Czechoslovakia, where he had established himself as a concert pianist, recitalist and recording artist. He settled in Toronto and made his recital debut at the University of Toronto, and

performed with the Toronto Symphony in 1969. Glenn Gould was one of his early supporters, and produced Kubálek's first commercial Canadian recording in 1973. His subsequent recordings of music from Mozart to Korngold, also includes compositions by Canadian composers. Kubálek's performance schedule includes chamber music and he has accompanied a number of singers. In addition to his duties as a teacher, he has been a record producer and liner-note writer for Dorian Records.

Kuerti, Anton
Although born in Austria, Anton Kuerti moved to the United States as a child, received his musical education there and established himself as an exceptional concert pianist following his professional debut in 1957. He decided to settle in Toronto in 1965. Kuerti has played with orchestras and given recitals throughout the world. He has toured extensively in Canada. Because of his personal beliefs and ideas about the presentation of music, he has taken an active role as a concert planner, as the founding artistic director of the Festival of the Sound and of Northstars Concerts, and recently as artistic adviser to Music Toronto. Kuerti's wide choice of repertoire is indicated by the long list of recordings which he has made, but he is recognized and admired particularly for his interpretations of the music of Beethoven. His virtuoso talents have gained him a well-deserved audience, and he is regarded as one of the outstanding pianists in Canada today. Kuerti has taught at the University of Toronto, and given many master classes. He espouses a number of political and environmental causes. These convictions led him to run in the 1988 federal election as an NDP candidate.

Lachapelle, Guy
This well-known Montreal percussionist, who joined the Montreal Symphony Orchestra in 1954 and served as the principal of the section for twenty years, is also a composer and a teacher. He was active in the Montreal jazz community in the early 1960s and helped run a nightclub. He augmented his work with the Société de musique contemporaine du Québec, with which he performed, by becoming a director in 1968. As a composer he has prepared or collaborated in the preparation of scores for modern dance companies. Lachapelle has taught at Montreal's Conservatoire de musique.

Lagacé, Bernard CM
The organist, harpsichordist and teacher Bernard Lagacé pursued his musical studies in his native St. Hyacinthe, Quebec, in Montreal, Paris and Vienna. A member of a well-known musical family, Lagacé is himself recognized internationally as an organ recitalist. A specialist in music of the baroque period, particularly that of J.S. Bach, he has performed in Europe, the United States and Canada. Lagacé is highly respected as a teacher and has been in demand as a juror for

national and international competitions. He has been influential in the rekindling of interest in the classical organ on this continent. He is married to Mireille Lagacé.

Lagacé, Mireille
Mireille Bégin Legacé was born in St-Jérôme Quebec, and studied piano, organ and theory in Montreal before winning a Quebec scholarship that allowed her to go to Austria for further organ studies. She then worked in Montreal with Bernard Lagacé, whom she later married. She was the recipient of a number of major international organ prizes, but the harpsichord has been an important part of her career as a soloist and a chamber musician. She has performed on both instruments in Canada, the United States and Europe. She teaches these instruments as well, and has had pupils in France and North America. Lagacé's extensive list of recordings includes a major portion of Bach's works for the harpsichord.

Lamon, Jean
Jean Lamon was born in New York city in 1949, and following her early violin studies, she began to investigate and then specialize in baroque violin performance. She gained valuable experience in this area with a number of groups in the United States. In 1981 Lamon joined the Toronto early music ensemble, Tafelmusik, which had been founded in 1978. By the mid-1980's this period instrument orchestra was becoming internationally recognized for the precision of its ensemble, its vitality, its repertoire, and the authenticity of its approach to the performance of early music. The group's success has coincided with the rapid growth of interest in the authentic performance movement in North America and in Europe. As Tafelmusik's music director, Lamon leads the orchestra from the concertmaster's chair, and has overseen its development into a full-time professional ensemble — one whose excellent reputation has been heightened by its many tours (in Canada, Europe and the Far East), and its long list of recordings that receive world-wide distribution. Lamon and Tafelmusik perform regularly in Toronto and many of its performances are broadcast.

Laplante, André
André Laplante's career as a pianist of international stature blossomed after he shared the silver medal at Moscow's famed International Tchaikovsky Competition in 1978, where he had been the favorite of the audience. The young soloist from Rimouski Quebec had studied in Montreal, at New York's Juilliard School, and in Paris; and had also won prizes in a number of other competitions. But it was his popular acclaim in Russia that earned him many concert engagements, important recital tours and festival appearances throughout the world. Laplante has performed at Carnegie Hall, has given recitals with the violinist Yehudi Menuhin, and also per-

forms as a member of the André-Laplante Trio. In addition to his performances in Europe, the United States and the East, he has played many times with orchestras throughout Canada.

Laurie, Ronald
Cellist Ronald Laurie has been a member of the Toronto Symphony for thirty-eight years, and assistant principal of the section for more than half that time. Born in Toronto, he studied at the Conservatory with Charles Mathé, then Isaac Mammott (both of whom were members of the TSO, the latter principal for six years). Laurie also managed to commute to New York for lessons with Leonard Rose. In addition to his work with the symphony, Laurie has been a member of the Halifax Symphony, and the National Ballet of Canada orchestra; played as a member of the orchestras at the Stratford Festival and with the Canadian Opera Company; and was an original member of the Hart House Orchestra with conductor Boyd Neel. He has been a long-time member of the in-school ensembles sponsored by the Toronto Symphony Education Programmes.

Lortie, Louis OC
Regarded as an outstanding and gifted pianist of his generation, Louis Lortie was born in Montreal in 1959, studied there with Yvonne Hubert, in Europe and in the United States. He had won a number of awards before he was asked to appear as soloist with the Toronto Symphony during its 1978 tour of China and Japan. Additional prizes in the Busoni and Leeds competitions brought his name to international attention in 1984. Lortie has continued to develop his career with recital tours and concert appearances in Europe, Canada and the United States. He has made award-winning recordings, and has been praised particularly for his performance of the music of Liszt and Ravel. He has recorded all of the latter's works for solo piano, and together with pianist Hélène Mercier, his music for piano four hands. At this time he is recording all of the Beethoven sonatas. Lortie was the pianist chosen to inaugurate the Glenn Gould Studio in the new CBC building in Toronto in 1992.

Louie, Alexina
Alexina Louie is one of the new generation of Canadian composers whose works have gained a reputation both in Canada and abroad. Born in Vancouver in 1949, Louie studied piano and composition both there and in California. She earned a master's degree in 1974 from the University of California at San Diego, and she made a special study of the music of the Orient. She taught at the city colleges of Pasedena and Los Angeles until she settled in Toronto in 1980. From that time she focused her energies on composition, and has received a number of important commissions. Her works for orchestra and for chamber ensembles display her use of more traditional forms and structures with the language and techniques of the later twentieth century, and she explores the

sonorities that are reminiscent of the music of the East. Her music can be atmospheric, evocative at one moment and rhythmic and highly percussive the next. She is a founding director of the Esprit Orchestra—a group conducted by her husband Alex Pauk—that is dedicated to the commissioning and performance of contemporary works.

Maestrini, Carlo
This Italian stage director was responsible for a number of operatic productions in Montreal, including eight for the Ópera du Québec during the four seasons of the company's existence in the early 1970s. Maestrini was also the stage director for the outstanding production by the Montreal Symphony Orchestra, of *Othello*, with Jon Vickers and Louis Quilico, that was part of the World Festival at Expo 67.

Mansouri, Lotfi
Iranian-born Lotfi Mansouri succeeded Herman Geiger-Torel as General Director of the Canadian Opera Company in 1976. During his twelve-year tenure a number of important changes and developments occurred for the company. It began to spread its productions throughout the year, rather than have them occur in only one season; it established the Canadian Opera Company Ensemble to train young Canadian singers; and it set up a composers-in-residence programme. Mansouri was the stage director for sixty-six productions of forty-two operas. New and lesser-known operas were added to the company's repertoire. He guided its affairs with enthusiasm, administrative skill and great energy. Mansouri became the director of the San Francisco Opera in 1990.

Marr, Frances CM
Born in Ridgetown, Ontario in 1900, Frances Marr studied piano in Toronto where she met and married the violinist Harry Adaskin. For forty-six years the pair performed as a piano-violin duo, giving recitals throughout Canada, in the United States, in Europe and on radio broadcasts. When her husband retired from performance in 1969, Marr continued to accompany and partner other instrumentalists and singers.

Marshall, Lois CC
When the Toronto-born and trained soprano Lois Marshall won the 1952 Naumberg Award in New York City, the world discovered and demanded to hear an extraordinary voice—one which had been enchanting and electrifying Toronto audiences since Sir Ernest MacMillan had engaged Marshall to sing in the *St. Matthew Passion* in 1947. Her long international career took her around the globe. She sang with the great orchestras, the best conductors, the outstanding choirs and singers of the times. She gave solo recitals, was a member of the famed Bach Aria Group of New York for fifteen years, made recordings and broadcasts, performed at festivals (Glenn Gould was her accompanist at Stratford in 1962), and appeared in

some opera productions. In the mid-1970s Marshall began to sing as a mezzo and gave some memorable performances, particularly of Lieder. She has now retired from performance, but continues to share her sensitive musical understanding and knowledge with her pupils at the University of Toronto.

Maule, Carolyn

Pianist Carolyn Maule is a native of Parry Sound, Ontario. She studied piano in Toronto with Marietta Orloff, both at the Royal Conservatory and at the University of Toronto. She performs as an accompanyist with many musicians, and singers (including her husband, Russell Braun). She is on the staff at the Faculty of Music in Toronto, as an assistant to Greta Kraus in her Lieder classes. Maule has been a regular participant at the concerts of the annual Festival of the Sound, which is based in her home town.

McDonall, Lois

Soprano Lois McDonall became an overnight operatic sensation when she took over the title role in Handel's *Semele* on very short notice, at the Sadler's Wells Opera. The Alberta-born singer had studied at the University of Toronto with Irene Jessner and had sung with the Canadian Opera Company before assuming leading roles for a season in Flensburg, Germany, prior to joining the Sadler's Wells company in London in 1969. She remained a resident artist there until 1984. Among her many parts, she created the title role in Iain Hamilton's opera *Anna Karenina* in 1981. McDonall made many guest appearances with the opera companies in Great Britain and in Canada. She began teaching at the Royal Conservatory and at the University of Toronto following her return to Toronto 1984.

McKay, James

Bassoonist, conductor and educator James McKay was born in Toronto in 1944, studied at the University of Toronto, then at Indiana University and at the University of Chicago. A committed chamber musician, he has been a member of a number of ensembles including the York Winds, and has made repeated appearances with the Festival of the Sound's Festival Winds. McKay was the Chairman of the Music Department at York University for six years before being appointed Chairman of Applied Music at the University of Western Ontario.

Montgomery, James

In 1972 this Ohio native received his master's degree from the University of Toronto, where he had studied composition with John Weinzweig and Gustave Ciamaga. He remained in Toronto, and became one of the founding members of the Canadian Electronic Ensemble. In addition to his work as a composer, in which he has continued to use and explore electronic technology and a variety of media to supplement more traditional instrumentation, Montgomery has been an administrator and artistic director for New Music Concerts and the Music Gallery. He began teaching at the University of Toronto in 1990.

Morawetz, Oskar CM

When Oskar Morawetz was forced by the circumstances of war to leave Czechoslovakia, he chose Canada as his refuge, and settled in Toronto in 1940. He continued his musical education (begun in Prague and Vienna) at the University of Toronto, where, by 1946 he was a faculty member. A distinguished teacher, he guided and helped develop the skills of music pupils until his retirement in 1982. It is, however, as a composer—one of Canada's "most performed" composers—that Morawetz is best known by the musical public, and his reputation extends far beyond our borders. Several of his large works have received major awards, and many have been written on commission. All of his compositions are characterized by a strong emotional appeal, and at times—as in *From the Diary of Anne Frank*—by an intense and dark dramatism that borders on the tragic. He has achieved this without using avant-garde or serial techniques, but by his skilled use of orchestral color, by his ability to weld emotional ends to the musical means at hand. A high proportion of his extensive list of compositions has been recorded.

Nelsova, Zara

This internationally renowned cellist, who has enjoyed a long and rewarding career as a concert and recording artist, was born in Winnipeg, where she received her early musical training from her father. She first performed there in a trio with her sisters who played violin and piano. This trio continued to perform publicly after the family moved to England. It was in London that Nelsova made both her solo recital and concert debuts. She returned to Canada in 1939, was principal cello with the Toronto Symphony Orchestra for several years, and formed a remarkable trio with violinist Kathleen Parlow and pianist Sir Ernest MacMillan. Nelsova became an American citizen in 1953, but she has continued to return to Canada to perform, give master classes and appear on radio and television. Her verve and joy in the music she performs with such skill and strength, have made her a favorite with audiences, conductors and orchestras wherever she has played. She lives in New York.

Orford String Quartet

In August 1965, four young Canadian string players, coached by Lorand Fenyves, gave a concert at the Orford Arts Center in Quebec. The Orford String Quartet was launched on its distinguished twenty-six-year journey into the international world of chamber music performance. The original members were violinists Andrew Dawes (born in High River, Alberta), Kenneth Perkins (born in Brockville, Ontario), violist Terence Helmer (born in Kirkland Lake, Ontario), and cellist Marcel Saint-Cyr (born in Quebec City). Denis Brott replaced Saint-Cyr in 1980. Throughout much of its career, the Orford was quartet-in-residence at the University of Toronto, but it was also active in training young string players at conservatories, schools, and universities across Canada. The Orford performed more than 180 works, from the classical to the contemporary periods, including many compositions by Canadian composers. It was critically acclaimed wherever it played, for its elegant, fluid style, and its consistently high level of ensemble. One of the best-known and long lived Canadian chamber groups, it has left a legacy of many excellent recordings.

Oundjian, Peter

The peripatetic life of a concert violinist has taken Toronto-born Peter Oundjian around the world. He studied first in London at the Royal College of Music, then in New York, where he graduated from Juilliard with both his bachelor and master's degrees. He has appeared as a soloist with many Canadian orchestras, and in 1981 became the first violinist of the internationally known Tokyo String Quartet. Oundjian continues to pursue a career as both a soloist and as a chamber musician. He makes his home in Connecticut.

Ozolins, Arthur

Arthur Ozolins' first Canadian teacher was composer Talivaldis Kenins—the first of several Torontonians who assisted the young pianist. Ozolins had been brought to the city after twelve years of displacement and insecurity (of Latvian heritage, he was born in a refugee camp in Germany in 1946, then lived in Argentina). Both his mother and grandmother had been concert pianists, and he was determined to undertake a musical career. He made his Toronto Symphony concert debut in 1961, when he was fifteen. His musical education continued with Alberto Guerrero in Toronto, Nadia Boulanger in Paris, then with Nadia Reisenberg in New York, before he began a truly professional career that has taken him to countries and continents around the globe. He has performed more than fifty times with the Toronto Symphony—and also made recordings with it—has been a welcomed and acclaimed soloist in the USSR, South America, the United States, Australia, and in Europe has developed a strong following in Sweden. Ozolins is praised for the vigorous, yet graceful style of his interpretations of the technically demanding works of such composers as Rachmaninoff and Prokoviev. Always aware of his own background, he has been a champion and exponent of the music of Latvian composers.

Pelletier, Wilfrid CC

Wilfrid Pelletier was born in Montreal in 1896 and had a varied music education as a pianist and a percussionist. He won Quebec's Prix d'Europe in 1915 and travelled to Paris for two years of study with pianist Isidor Philipp and Charles-Marie Widor. However, it was his move to New York—which became his life-long home—that led to his long and rewarding association with the Metropolitan Opera. By 1922 he was an assistant conductor; from 1929 to 1950, a regular conductor. It was Pelletier who conceived the Met's "Auditions of the Air" broadcasts, which have launched so many young singers (for example Canadians Quilico, Forst and Heppner). Nor was Pelletier's conducting limited to that house. He appeared with a number of other companies and as an orchestral conductor. In 1934 he became the first artistic director of the newly established Montreal Symphony Orchestra. He quickly set up a series of young people's concerts, and became the chief organizer of the Montreal Festival. Then to crown his contribution to music and youth in his native province, he was pivotal in setting up the Conservatoire de musique et d'art dramatique in 1943, and was its director until 1961. Pelletier lived in New York until his death in 1982.

Quilico, Gino OC

It seemed inevitable that Gino Quilico would sing. If your father, Louis, is an international opera star, and your mother, Lina, is an accomplished pianist and vocal coach, then music is the family business. However, success in an operatic career required something more than naturally good vocal chords or inherited talent. Baritone Gino Quilico, born in New York in 1955, studied with both his parents, at the University of Toronto Opera School, and at the school of the Paris Opera. He began his professional career in a Toronto COMUS Music Theatre production in 1977; has sung with the Canadian Opera Company, in Montreal, at Covent Garden, in European houses and at the Metropolitan Opera. He and his father Louis have appeared together in the Canadian Opera Company's 1979 *Simon Boccanegra*, and its 1988 *Don Giovanni*, and at the Met in *Manon* in 1991—a rare achievement for any father-son team. Gino Quilico was one of three Canadian singers (Teresa Stratas and Tracey Dahl were the other two) who sang in the premiere of John Corigliano's new opera *The Ghosts of Versailles* in 1991 at the Metropolitan. He has gained his own place in the world of international opera.

Quilico, Louis CC

Baritone Louis Quilico began singing as a solo chorister in his native Montreal, where he was born in 1925. He studied there, in Rome and New York, and began winning vocal competitions, including the Metropolitan Opera Auditions of the Air in 1955, after he had made his professional opera debut in Montreal in 1954. Quilico's outstanding career as an operatic singer of power, who possesses a richly colored and dramatic voice, has been conducted in all the world's great opera houses and with many companies in

Canada. Although less frequent now, his concert and oratorio appearances have delighted concert audiences and critics alike. In addition to his long and distinguished singing career, in a wide range of roles, Quilico taught for seventeen years at the faculty of music at the University of Toronto, and for three years at McGill.

Robbin, Catherine

Mezzo-soprano Catherine Robbin is often regarded as a specialist in the baroque repertoire. She has performed and recorded with Tafelmusik, and with conductors John Eliot Gardiner, Christopher Hogwood and Trevor Pinnock, in much of this music, for which her rich, cleanly and evenly focused voice is well suited. However, this Toronto-born singer is a performer of the classical and contemporary music as well. She studied in Toronto, Vancouver, the United States and in England, making her professional concert debut in 1972 in *Messiah* with the St. Catharines' Symphony Orchestra. She subsequently won several major vocal awards, and has enjoyed a career that includes recital and concert engagements in Canada and abroad, and some appearances in opera—both staged and in concert.

Rolston, Shauna

The cellist Shauna Rolston showed exceptional talent at a young age. Born into a musical family—her father Thomas is a violinist, her mother Isobel, a pianist—in Edmonton in 1967, she studied with Claude Kenneson and at Yale University. Her seemingly effortless technique and natural command of her instrument and its repertoire have allowed her to make the transition from gifted child to mature artist with ease. She enjoys performing as a soloist with orchestras, as a chamber musician, and on radio and television broadcasts. She began making recordings in the mid-1980s. She was appointed an assistant professor at the University of Toronto in 1994.

Roslak, Roxolana

One of the unforgettable moments in the first production of Harry Somers' opera *Louis Riel* was an unaccompanied lullaby, "Kuyas", sung with intense poignancy by a young soprano, Roxolana Roslak. She had been born in the Ukraine, came to Canada as a child, and had studied voice in Edmonton and Toronto, graduating from the University of Toronto in 1964. After her role as Marguerite (which she repeated in the opera's 1975 revival), she continued to appear with the Canadian Opera Company, sang with Opera in Concert, with orchestras across Canada, and as a soloist with the Toronto Mendelssohn Choir. She made a memorable CBC TV appearance in 1975 with Glenn Gould as pianist in Hindemith's *Das Marienleben*, which they also recorded. She has commissioned and premiered vocal works of several Canadian composers. Roslak began teaching at the Royal Conservatory in 1986.

St. John, Scott

This young violinist represents a new generation of string instrumentalists. He was born in 1969 in London, Ontario and began studying there when he was three. His teachers have included Richard Lawrence, Ralph Aldrich and Gérard Jarry in Paris. He continued at the Cleveland Institute and at Curtis in Philadelphia. By 1990 St. John had won a number of competitions in Canada and the United States. He has performed as a guest soloist with orchestras in England and North America, and gave recitals under the auspices of Jeunesses musicales in Europe and England. He made his Carnegie Recital Hall debut in 1988.

St. Lawrence Quartet

The four young musicians who formed a string quartet in the autumn of 1989 in Toronto, quickly established a reputation as one of the important ensembles of the 1990s. Following a year of supervision and coaching with Lorand Fenyves and Denis Brott at the University of Toronto and the Royal Conservatory of Music, the quartet was appointed to a two-year residency at the Hartt School of Music in Connecticut, where the members worked with the Emerson Quartet. Violinists Geoff Nuttal and Barry Shiffman, violist Lesley Robertson and cellist Marina Hoover were also honored with residency appointments to the Juilliard School in New York. The quartet's many performances in recital are marked by a distinctive, passionate style, and this musical command and intensity has earned it top awards at the Melbourne International Chamber Music Competition in Australia, the Glory of Mozart Competition in St. John's, and the prestigious first place at the Banff International Quartet Competition in 1992. The quartet has performed in the United States, Europe and Canada, at summer festivals, and on the CBC. In 1994, it was named quartet-in-residence at the University of Toronto.

Saraste, Jukka-Pekka

The Toronto Symphony announced the appointment of Jukka-Pekka Saraste as its new music director in 1993, effective at the start of the 1994-5 season. The young Finnish conductor, who was born in Heinola in 1956, has had a thorough musical education in his native country. He studied piano, violin, and, with the encouragement of his teachers, began conducting when he was only twelve. By 1987 he had become the principal conductor of the Finnish Radio Symphony Orchestra and of Edinburgh's Scottish Chamber Orchestra. He has toured and made recordings with both of these ensembles. Saraste and his family settled in Toronto in 1994 as he began the first year of his tenure as the eighth music director of the Toronto Symphony Orchestra.

Schafer, R. Murray

R. Murray Schafer is a composer, a dramatist, an educator, a writer, a music-literary-linguistic scholar, and a visual artist, as well as a pioneer in the study of the sonic landscape. He is, and is internationally recognized as, a veritable renaissance man— largely self-taught. He was born in Sarnia, Ontario in 1933. Although he studied music at the University of Toronto, he did not complete the course, but chose to travel and study in Europe and England. When he returned to Canada he taught, first in Newfoundland, then in British Columbia. In 1975 he settled in rural south-eastern Ontario. Some of Schafer's multimedia musical-theatrical works exemplify his belief in the community as the basis of the creative process; others of his compositions combine the natural elements of landscape with instruments that produce sound-music. He often composes on commission, for a variety of instruments, and instrumental forces, producing music that is highly personal, original and compelling. As an educator, Schafer has written extensively for both student and scholar. He has called himself "the father of acoustic ecology" and has published several books and many articles on the subject of our contemporary, often intrusive and harmful, soundscape. His achievements in his multi-facted creative life have been recognized with a number of honors and awards, but Schafer continues to defy categorization or limitation of any sort.

Schenkman, Peter

A graduate of the Curtis Institute in Philadelphia, where he studied with Leonard Rose, cellist Peter Schenkman served in the United States army band, then joined the Boston Symphony in 1962. He was also on the performing staff at the Marlboro Musical Festival. He settled in Toronto in the late 1960s and became principal cellist of the Toronto Symphony, a position he held for seven seasons. Schenkman has carried on a busy career in Toronto as a performer, orchestral player, contractor, studio musician, and chamber musician. He has also taught and coached with the National Youth Orchestra and at the Royal Conservatory of Music.

Somers, Harry CC

From the time that Harry Somers determined to pursue his musical career as a composer, rather than as a pianist, he has composed prolifically. Somers is regarded as one of Canada's most important creative artists, and his music has received international recognition and performance. His versatility and ease in using the new, as well as the traditional forms and techniques, have assured him many commissions. Long, fluid lines, the sensitive manipulation of rhythm, and the skillful use of dynamic changes—are all characteristic of his work. His interest in the human voice, and the effects that may be used to exploit—or extend—its capabilities, is evident in his work, whether the compositions be large-scaled opera or musical theater (*Louis Riel*, *Serinete*), or for choirs or solo voices. In addition, Somers has composed with distinction in every genre: film, opera, ballet, television, for orchestra, soloists with orchestra, for a variety of chamber ensembles, large and small, and he has composed fluently for piano. Fortunately many of his compositions have been recorded. Somers, who was born in Toronto in 1925, continues to make his home in that city.

Stratas, Teresa OC

Born in Toronto of Greek parents, the soprano Teresa Stratas made an acclaimed operatic debut as Mimi in the Canadian Opera Company's 1958 production of *La Bohème*. She was twenty. This was followed quickly by her debut at the Metropolitan Opera in 1959. Over the next decades, this intelligent, intense, musically impeccable singer performed at the famed opera houses of Europe and North America, in the leading soprano roles of Mozart, Rossini, Bizet, Puccini, Verdi and Tchaikovsky. As well, conductors and directors have sought her to help create contemporary, often dramatically demanding, characters. Pierre Boulez chose her to sing the title role in the first complete performance of Alban Berg's *Lulu* in Paris 1979. North American opera lovers experienced her vocal and dramatic art in the television broadcast of the Met's premiere of John Coringliano's *The Ghosts of Versailles* in 1991. Her recordings of Kurt Weill's songs reveal another aspect of Stratas' sensitive communicative powers.

Sukis, Lilian

Lyric soprano Lilian Sukis, born in Lithuania, moved to Hamilton, Ontario in 1950. She earned her artist's diploma from the University of Toronto in 1965, and credits Arnold Walter, Irene Jessner and Greta Kraus as the guides who directed the development of her voice and musical sensibility. Sukis appeared with the Canadian Opera Company and with the Metropolitan Opera before deciding that she would make her career in Europe. In 1969 she joined the Munich State Opera. She has since performed with conductors such as von Karajan, Böhm and Sawallish, in major opera houses in Germany and Austria, in leading roles in operas by Mozart, Debussy and Strauss. She gave the 1972 premiere of *Sim Tjong*, which Korean composer Isang Yun composed for her. Sukis returns occasionally to Canada to give recitals of Lieder, or to sing as a guest artist in concert or in opera.

Tremblay, Gilles

The composer Gilles Tremblay is regarded as one of the leaders of the avant-garde in Quebec. Following studies in Montreal and at Marlboro in Vermont, he spent five years in Paris. There he perfected his skills as an ondist. studying with Martenot himself, and began to develop what became a life-long interest in electro-acoustic techniques and the nature of sound. The analysis and the use of pitch, rhythm and sonic resonance have become hallmarks of his compositions. His mentors in Paris included Stockhausen and Boulez. Tremblay prepared the prize-winning sound tracks for the Quebec pavillion at Expo 67. His compositions have earned international recognition, and he has continued to receive commissions from organizations in Canada and abroad. In addition to his valuable contribution as a board member and his administrative work, Tremblay has served as a jury member for composition and performance competitions.

Tsutsumi, Tsuyoshi
Following his youthful studies in Tokyo, where he was born in 1942, cellist Tsutsumi made his debut at age twelve. He determined to study in the United States, and he won a number of important performance competitions as his international career developed. Tsutsumi has long had a Canadian connection. He has taught at the University of Western Ontario, at Toronto's Royal Conservatory, given master classes and workshops at many summer schools, and been a respected juror at Canadian competitions. He has appeared as a guest soloist with Canadian orchestras, and has performed as a chamber musician—he was a founding member of Quartet Canada, and a member of the Hidy-Ozolins-Tsutsumi Trio. His long list of recordings includes a number of works by Canadian composers.

Vickers, Jon CC
Jon Vickers did not undertake formal vocal studies until he was twenty-four, when he entered Toronto's Royal Conservatory in 1950. Born in Prince Albert, Saskatchewan, he had sung in choirs and amateur musical productions. By the mid-1950's he had established a strong, but local, reputation for his concert, oratorio and opera performances. In 1956 he was asked to audition for the Royal Opera, Covent Garden and given a contract. In 1958 he achieved European recognition when he sang Siegmund in his Bayreuth debut. During his long and illustrious international career, Vickers sang most of the dramatic and Heldentenor roles in all the world's leading opera houses. He was renown for the robust, tireless, intensely dramatic quality of his tenor voice. In his great roles—for example in *Peter Grimes*—he was able to articulate in sound the inarticulate emotions behind the character's actions and words. Vickers had a long association with conductor Herbert von Karajan, with whom he made many of his operatic recordings. Although Vickers' operatic appearances were rare in Canada, he did give a number of recitals there, and indeed sang his first *Winterreise* at the Guelph Spring Festival in 1979. He announced his retirement in 1988.

Washburn, Jon
When Jon Washburn moved from his native Illinois to Vancouver in 1965, he undertook a variety of musical activities, including performance on such early instruments as viol da gamba and violone, conducting choral groups, and composing and arranging music for choir. He was a

founding member of the Vancouver Society for Early Music, and has been co-artistic director of the Masterpiece Chamber Music Series. However, it is his work as a choral director of a number of groups—the Vancouver Chamber Choir, the Amity Singers, the Ladies' Bach Choir—that has earned him the recognition and respect of his musical peers, and the admiration of audiences, whether at home in Vancouver or during his tours and guest conducting assignments throughout Canada.

Wiens, Edith
Born into a Mennonite family in Saskatoon, soprano Edith Wiens grew up in Vancouver, studied there, and in Germany, and received a masters degree in music from Oberlin College in Ohio. Her career as a concert artist and recitalist has taken her throughout the world, and she has performed with all the leading conductors. Wiens made her operatic debut at Glyndbourne in 1986. Although she makes her home in Germany, she returns to sing in Canada in concert, recital and in oratorio performances. Her many recordings indicate her preference for the music of Bach, Hadyn and Mozart. Her lyric soprano is also well-suited to the vocal works of Brahms, Schubert, Schumann and Strauss.

Weinzweig, John OC
It is impossible in a few lines, to summarize or evaluate the musical career and influence of composer, teacher and administrator John Weinzweig, who was born in Toronto in 1913, and who in 1994, continues to be a creative force in the Canadian musical community. He studied at the University of Toronto, then at the Eastman School in Rochester, New York. At the latter he was exposed to some of the new compositional theories and techniques. Weinzweig was the first Canadian composer to explore twelve-tone composition, and as a teacher—at both the Royal Conservatory and the University of Toronto—he introduced his pupils to twentieth-century music concepts and principles. He was a founder of the Canadian League of Composers, serving two terms as its president. He is a prolific composer of music in many genres—many film scores, ballet music, music for orchestra, for band, for soloists with orchestra, and for a daunting range of chamber groups and combinations of instruments. Some of his works, normally characterized by a rhythmic vitality and a clean, economic texture, display a wry wit and humor, and at times he uses the vocabulary of the world of jazz and pop music. Others of his works indicate the depth of his humanitarianism, his dedication to the ideals of the cooperative spirit. He has been the subject of films, television specials, books and articles, and has received honors and awards in recognition of his lifelong contribution to the life of music and mankind.

Afterword

Louis Applebaum

IN THE LAST FIVE OR SIX DECADES, Canadian musical artists have turned up on our stages in surprising numbers to provide us with creations and performances of remarkable quality. Some have achieved world-wide reputations and have been well-applauded everywhere. Others, while achieving attention abroad, have found that at home the respect accorded them was casual, if not indifferent. This volume should help counterbalance a self-effacement that may be a common national trait but is contrary to the interests of performers and other artists in need of appreciation and attention.

CBC radio, at least until recently, has been a constant and vital intermediary between our musicians and their audiences. Essential as this may have been in our artistic evolution, it has left our musicians faceless and distant. Composers, especially, have remained incognito, contacting their audiences only during the few seconds when they stand up in a concert hall to acknowledge the applause after a performance of one of their works. Those who try to catch a glimpse of the author of the work (too often for the first and only time) see only a distant figure waving his hand at the performer before disappearing again into obscurity.

Walter Curtin, through his unususal photographer's eye, has given us an opportunity to make close contact with our musicians in studios, concert hall dressing rooms, during rehearsals, and in their homes. Often we can hide behind the invisible curtain to watch as they are in the process of making or preparing the music we enjoy and savor. For once, we have the opportunity to see our musicians not through a formal portrait or on a distant stage but through a close-up that is revealing and memorable.

To see Glenn Gould, crouched over a piano, capped and scarved, lost in the intensity of his work and oblivious to everything else, is to meet him in a way that even a Gould concert cannot offer. To visit Teresa Stratas in her home, hiding her face in embarassment, is to see her in a self-revealing pose that tells us, privately, so much more than even a lengthy interview would disclose.

The current generation sometimes has trouble accepting the fact that not too long ago we had only meagre artistic resources. Outside the largest cities, there were no opera, ballet or dance companies, and in those cities, quasi-professional orchestras played short seasons. The few composers among us usually made a living as church organists or teachers. There was no indigenous theatre— so only rarely were plays written for performance and then by the amateur companies of the day. Now we number our composers and writers in the hundreds, local opera and ballet companies play in cities across the whole expanse of Canada, our singers and instrumentalists are equal to the best anywhere, and symphony orchestras and chamber ensembles abound. Music schools have been able to prepare the performers and composers who can satify more and more of our musical ambitions, making it less necessary to import talent for our pleasure and edification.

The first *Encyclopedia of Music in Canada* was compiled and published in 1981and it was1,000 pages. This volume by Walter Curtin has no encyclopedic aspiration. Out of the 30,000 photos that Curtin has taken of musicians, only a precious handfull have found their way into this book. Our musical artists have never been paid tribute in this way. Perhaps others will be inspired to acknowledge forthcoming generations in a similar vein. In the meantime, we have a treasure to cherish, a way of applauding the high standards and achievments of our musician players, singers and writers.

To Walter Curtin, for his dedication, persistence, craft, vision and artistry, our thanks.